Elements of Love & Drama

Miss Dee

authorHOUSE®

AuthorHouse™
1663 Liberty Drive, Suite 200
Bloomington, IN 47403
www.authorhouse.com
Phone: 1-800-839-8640

First published by AuthorHouse 3/17/2009

ISBN: 978-1-4389-6002-9 (sc)

Printed in the United States of America
Bloomington, Indiana

This book is printed on acid-free paper.

<u>Dedication</u>

This book is dedicated to my son that is now in heaven watching over me. You will forever be missed by all of us I love you sweet Maalik. Also to my parents that's also is in heaven shining on my everyday. I know they watch me and are the reason I became a published author.

Table of Contents

The Preface

This is a book of Poetry that is intended for everyone whom has experienced "Love and Drama" at its best or its worst. While this subject is worldwide, this book approaches many situations and circumstances that we face and overcome on a daily basis. This book of Poetry was originated from my inner thoughts and feelings I have sprinkled it with a few spices that will make you both, cry and laugh. These pages were put together for Men and Woman whom have experienced life at it's Core and is trying to overcome, or has been successful in overcoming the obstacles that we all face. There is no color, origin, or sexuality on Love and Drama and its Elements, attached to it. In conclusion, after reading and experiencing the spoken words and true poetry on the pages ahead, you will be enlightened and intrigued how Love and all of its Drama can help you to overcome and achieve any thing that you put your mind to.

<u>Acknowledgements</u>

First in foremost I'd like to give praise to the Almighty God.
Without him I would not be here. To my husband thank you for always keeping my cool and mind elevated. To my parents that's no longer here thanks for always guiding me in the right direction. To my children thank you for always keeping me on my toes, I love you. I also want to give thanks to my little light you know who you are. My sister Michelle AKA Tweet thanks you for the encouragement and wisdom. In a time of not having my mother you give me a constant reminder she is with me. My best friend Alexis, thank you for being a true friend. We been through a lot together and neither of us ever turned away I love you. To Doris my mother in Law...We had a rough start until we allowed ourselves to know one another. You are an inspiration thanks for being there. To my uncle Tony you always had a positive attitude towards me thanks for sharing those memories of my mother I never known. To my nephew Marcus, you had faith in me when others turned their backs. Thanks for knowing the true me. To my man a hundred grand Eric AKA E&J, thanks for being a brother from another mother! To Antwoine thanks for always telling me I would never amount to anything. That statement was my motivation to keep going! My family members that do care thanks for being there you know who you are. If the shoe doesn't fit please don't wear it. To my www.blogtalkradio.com family & my groups on Black planet (Black Women Poetry) & www.poetryafterdarknl. ning.com, you are the vessel of my poetry thank you for the encouragement and the love shown for my writing.

Some of you made a huge impression on me: Dymon-J, The Nxt Lvl, Philly-Stylez, Prophecy, Sun of Man, Lady Blue, Eryk Moore, Geovannimercal, Cambridge Jenkins, Spicy, LyriQ and a host of others thank you. To Shelvan my friend thank you for always being there we are going 12 years strong.

A Friend
By Miss~Dee

A friend is to stay by your side...
In a friend you know you can confide...
A listener when in need...
This is one that would never mislead...

Love came to my finesse
My Grace,
My Elegance!

Then innovation became romance...
Enhanced with friendship...

We're becoming too close...
Daydreaming...
Of
Stripping Clothes...

A friend...

This sensation grows...
It's not a daisy but more like a rose...
Like water this friend helps me grow...

As our conversation strengthens
In you I know you're the one to listen
You are the solar to my glisten...

A friend...

In the mind, it captures ruin...
But...you're the channel I'm viewing...

I'm taking steps to pursue what is wrong...
Incoherent the mind runs long...
You feel it we feel it, you and I belong...

A friend...

The line has been crossed...
Not realizing this friendship could be lost
Am I willing to pay the cost?

I'm so infatuated with this...
In denial, because I can't believe it exists...
This makes it hard to resist...
All caught up in Lustful bliss...

Lover...

Even if it just for a short time...
My body is what I want to assign...
And remain blinded to the truth....

The ecstasy is strong within...
You and me
This is where it begins...
I will always be your friend...
You see in us there's no end...
The door remains open, so come in...

& Love me...

"Temptation can have a strong hold"

A Man's Treasure

By Miss Dee

A strong love had become domination...
Her eyes full of love's anticipation...
She's all caught up in this bizarre situation...

Her personal being is now his property...
He stole the innocence of her purity...
Secluded her surroundings to verbal abuse...
Furious mind but heart remained lingering...
Adhering to all that he said...

Inexperienced following him as he led...
Silent wishes tormented soul...
& now she's half of what was once whole...
Surrendered under his control...

He's not accepting the better half...
She still turns the other cheek and laugh...
Still making house a home...
Still doing it all alone...

But from the outside looking in
He's not even a friend
Let alone a husband...
He's just one to pretend

So Stop, don't defend
I want you to listen and comprehend
Your relationship must suspend
You can no longer commend....

His lies!
He denies his love for you...
He tries to steal the most precious thing too...
Your life!
So what you are his wife...

I know he supplies
But girl say goodbye...

In time love turns to despise
Heed to the wise...
There will be other guys...

You're going to miss your prize...
Accepting a man that chastise...

So, say you would never...
You are your own treasure
And I know you got this together...

Having real love brings,

Love,
Patience,
Kindness and
Honesty,

Wouldn't you all agree?
Real love is beauty!

"Verbal abuse can be just as harsh as physical"

All that I need
By: Miss Dee

Searching for something I don't need
I'm always starting back at one
I ignored that calm angelic spirit in me...
He was here before time begun...

The higher power beyond the sea...
The reason we have...
Apple trees...
A grass so green...
Stinging bumble bees...
A hot cup of herbal tea...
He is the reason...

The reason for living....
He forgives the unforgiving...
He is the true meaning to Thanksgiving...

But we all are sinners...
You know we haven't been here before...
So In life we all are beginners...

We're trying to live out our path...
Choose correctly overcome the wrath...
Think beyond the sight...
There's more there to endure...

Say:
Even though I walk through the valley of the shadow of
death...
I will fear no evil, for you are with me;

Your rod and your staff,
They comfort me.
That's what he wants us to see...

Basic instructions before leaving earth...
This is something your soul should be worth...
The beginning is your birth...

Live virtuous, ashes to ashes...
Dust to dust....
You see, it's that simple...
Your body is just a temple...
Savage your soul; bring peace to your mind...
God is love and love is blind!

"Our strength comes from within believe in Him"

Art of Seduction
By Miss Dee

Water glistening down my body...
You're eyes in position enjoying the vision
Mind blowing!

Lying relaxed from the Clench
You're drenched in the scent of me
I'm thirsting awaiting the quench

Time is of the essence
In receiving this blessing...

No Lights, No camera only Action

The art of seduction is put in production...
Please proceed with extreme caution...

There is no need for procrastinating...
I see that you are fascinated...
So the obligation is obliged....
Revel and indulged in this ride...

He is mandated to penetrate...
Longing as my soul aches
His hands on me as my legs shake...
Tongue in me as the rain pours...
So evolved in the reservoir....

Seductively, carefully formulated...
Highly, wisely, anticipated...

Where are we? Lost in space
Enjoying the taste of the most deluxe

Suck...Lick...and have me
The grasping of my waist...
Hold tight....
I'm Cumming on your face...

Amazed...
Again...he has risen

I will assume the position
Another vision of love...
Another mission of lust....
The Art of seduction is just.....

"When the mind can be seduced"

Dangerous
By Miss Dee

So I've tested the waters
Dipped and Dived...
The storm was strong but I survived...
In a constant need but deprived...

It's Dangerous...

I am investigating like a case
Still falling hard from grace...
I know there is an imposter
Watch as I proceed to chase...

I brace for a disaster...
Another matter...

Then situations erase...
I'm back at one...
Maybe even zero...
Searching for a long lost hero
Being at the bottom of the sun...
No fun no realization

It's Dangerous...

It's a manipulator of the mind
Abductor of the heart...
My soul cries because it wants to part...
Battery running dead
I need a jump start...

I'm lacking there of...
And still no love...
Going down I have to see the top
Flip flop

Damn!

Will this ever get right?
It's like black and white...
Grab at first sight,
I have no resistance to put up a fight....

It's Dangerous...

I'm leaping off a bridge
Not really using my head...
Just plain brain dead...

I'm blindfolded chained up...
Mission impossible I'm struck...
The force has its hold,
Its persistence is so cold...

It's Dangerous...

Do you know what it is?
No Sacredness...
Have you heard it like this?
No analysis...
Maybe this is too intense to absorb...
Soar!
Until you witness it remains in suspense...

It's Dangerous!!!

"Evil is always lurking around"

Deep Attraction
By Miss Dee

Intrigue by the presence of your words...
Writing for me is what you preferred...
Daydreaming of what could be...
What if we were free?

Free to love...
Free to embrace...

Locked in this empty space...
We crave for each other...
Tight ties with one another...
We still want to discover...

The intensity of our souls...
Living now waiting to unfold...
Making stories to be untold...
What we have is gold...

I am what you appeal...
It's too deep but so real...
We still have to conceal...
Many broken promises not to deal...

I want to feel...
I want to feel you inside of me...
Visit this passion at the sea...

It's guaranteed to make you believe...
The yearning I will relieve...
As we approach the point of no return...
Fiery souls and we burn

Only for you
I can only speak the truth!

All this waiting...
Role Playing...
Bodies aching...

It's mental love making...
Forsaken our bodies...

You have electrified my mind
All these emotions combined
Love and lust is confined
This is deep attraction of the mind!

"Making love to ones soul"

"Dream Sensitive"
By: Miss Dee

I'm walking with a strut...
I feel his eyes on my butt...
I can tell he's overjoyed...
Thinking.....I can be his toy....

So.....

Numbers we do exchange...
The players enter the game...
This dark seductive man...
Has my Juices flowing in my pants...

He will never know...
I leave things to guess...
Not for show...
Enter the game of chess...

Next....

I get a glimpse of what's to come...
He's so ready to have some...
I allow the lights to get dim...

I feel his hands moving up my thigh...
Oh my...He is not even shy...
His body and mine can't resist...
We engage in a lovely kiss...

Grasping...intertwined in a mist...
I feel warm and wet...
Body in a formation set...
I feel the entrance of him whole...

Speaking in tongue...
The vision of my soul...
There are words that can never unfold...

He's bounded by the sensation...
I'm amazed of the dedication...
To hearts create a space confined...
This is truly a dream, it's too genuine...

Now this next line is written for you...
Interview what you feel...
Reveal the true me...
Open what was closed down completely...

Your sensitive words...
Gestures from my black
Seductive lover...
I'm in tuned....
Waiting for another and another....

I've reached the mountain climax...
I'm not trying to be to direct...
You see, you have this affect...
Much respect you didn't neglect...

A woman that needed revival
You gave and I received until...

I turned...
Noticing the sun shine on me...
Astonished it was just a dream...

"Dreams can feel real too"

Dream

By Miss Dee

I will continue to dream
No matter how hard it may seem
I will not put down my pen
I know who's my closest friend
The one that has me open
Never to leave the heart broken

In reality I need this to be
I want to expand and have my own family tree
A legacy that was left by me
I know the territory of being envied
Mad at their own made destiny

I need to spread these wings
Open my heart and mind to new things
I want to scream and shout, rid myself of doubt
I want to be able to lift spirits
Become someone's dearest

You know given the opportunity I will succeed
Living life to the fullest indeed
A true way of my expression
Is always through this pen & paper
Got to shout out to the haters

My main reason for not giving up
I didn't run nor played a roll being stuck
I received mass blessings from the Lord
I had a great deal to absorb

Dealing with life trials and tribulations
Maybe now I can hear the words "congratulations"
Now listen to the emancipation of the poetic heart that sits in me
Let me spread my joy and let others finally see

2002

"A dream that was meant to come true"

Envy
By Miss Dee

In my eyes you were the intelligent one
To make ends meet you had to scramble
Therefore you couldn't afford the gamble
It seemed money was not your friend

Times grew hard not a soul to lend
Reality hits, you have mouths to feed
Won't allow the family to be in need
First thing to mind becomes entirely to risky

No worries to stand on your own two feet
The block was never a stranger to you
You had to make the necessary move
Things became cool like brand new

Your main man hated on the chief
Didn't appreciate your presence being so brief
Always said watch the company you keep
Keep the third eye and never sleep

His jealousy became devastating envy
Hand all out not appreciating his plenty
Or did he, haters will always be
Glad you woke up to finally see

Conquer those that trespass against
Don't talk about, but keep them in suspense
It's that kind that makes us who we are
Dilute the foulness and continue the preparation
You're going to find the right destination
To all those, you don't owe any explanation!

"Sometimes you have to do what's necessary to survive"

Four Walls
By Miss Dee

I am confined by these four walls...
Trapped and preparing for the downfall...
My voice as I speak sounds like a whisper...
Indulging life's pain in the bottle of liquor...

Stranger to myself; normal to someone else...
I can't identify the problem at hand...
Wishing to find the one that truly understands...
Seeking those ones I can't even reach...
I'll listen and bestow what he teaches...

Now being guided by this force of nature....
I apprehend what's behind the scenes...
I see the path the needs to be taken...
No longer will his love be forsaken...

So tired, tired of being torn...
I'll wait for the one that's worth the pursuit...
I'm straight forward little is needed to please...
Learning life knowing that it's no guarantees...

I'm not indigent don't need the validation...
Occasionally I yearn for some good conservation...
I am stepping out of this closed in space...
All the old memories from these walls erased...

Providing me with a fresh start...
Change is good especially from the heart...
Now the road less traveled is my mission...
Thank you, Lord this was the only decision!

"A breathe of fresh Air"

"Friendship Ruin"
By: Miss Dee

We were giving each other happiness...
Actually enduring the feeling of being blessed...
He granted me what I needed not wanted...
In my mind this could not be...

I grew to love his character....
All the other adversities didn't matter...
So I ask myself what went wrong.
This negative progression didn't take long...
Everything was like tranquility....Until

A part of me wasn't fully given....
Blinded to the fact....
This will be unforgiving....
Something I needed was missing...

I'm experiencing lust again....
My lover and friend....
Where do I begin?
I had what most strived life long for...

This sensation led me from
Loves anticipation...
Now this created foundation....
Has lost its salvation.....

I had it good....
The man understood...
He was like bread and Butter...
Still didn't stop me from the other...

I can't claim confused…
True lover I know I abused….
That physical hardcore…
Hit me hard never had it before…

I can't tell between….
What's the difference?
I enjoyed the experience…
My heart told my mind….
I ignored the proposition …

No this hard thought decision….
Hit me like a head on collision….
The friendship has been ruined…
There is nothing left for me to pursue…
I had enough…he had too much…
It's not just… My actions proved
I fucked up!

"Lustful endeavors not always what they seem"

Glass Soul

By Miss Dee

You really don't have to say much
Our lives were bonded in touch
I see more than you'll ever know
It's not necessary to have you here toe to toe

I know how you feel what your appeal is
You tried to break the tie that binds
I'm not the type to stay in your face
Not even the one to follow the chase

You gave me your eyes in its replace
You trying to explain to me is like watching
That movie "waiting to exhale" again

Your hands touch not what I remember
My eyes are the object to dismember
Factual presence no lie you can claim
Desperate fool thought you had the pussy tame

Shhh... Lost soul I see this is to advanced
Over time passing my perception enhanced
All the while you're thinking lack of experience
Let me teach you to tell the difference

What was done out there I already know
So why waste time and put off a show
I don't try to stereo type... No wouldn't be right
I just get my sixth sense when I observe you
Senses became better the emotions grew

You're still playing games acting a fool
Missing all the signs bending the rules
Still bringing mad fumes to the fuel
Well I may be still be moving to fast
The things I saw were from your soul of GLASS!!

"Actions speak louder than words"

"Going Round"
By Miss~Dee

You got me in the game at play...
Persuaded me to listen and stay...
We're going in circles everyday...
You speak on love but do not display...

You have another agenda...
I laid back and became the pretender...
My emotion flowed and surrenders...
Next I'm back being your contender...

Just going Round
My face in a frown
Our love comes down
I'm still hanging around...

Make up to break up...
I am not the chicken to be plucked...
I thought I was heart struck...
Back then as a young buck...

I let my heart speak for me...
Love as long as the ocean sea...
Undermining the no guarantee...

Just going Round
My face in a frown
Our love comes down
I'm still hanging around...

Should have known...
He wasn't on his own...
I am so afraid to be alone...
These issues became prone...

When there were others to bone...
When he whispered on the phone...
Then my love became disowned...

Just going Round
My face in a frown
Our love comes down
I'm still hanging around...

I'm through going round
I am grasping for solid ground...
My love is watered down...
And now my heart no longer pounds...

"When a women is fed up"

Got Up to Fall Down
By Miss Dee

Got up this morning noticed you weren't around
I listened heard you creeping, don't play clown
It's four a clock in the morning, ass out there boning
You're one tired ass nigga, out there doing what I figured

Just couldn't prove me wrong, chasing whores thong
Death becomes you trying to get into any & every
Enough, what you did was very voluntary
Now that the truth is out poof be gone
Here is not where you ever belonged...

Twenty minutes of ass left you homeless
Now you sit and stare at me heartless
You knew the deal when you did it
Leave please your face makes me sick

I'm not the one to become the other "Female"
Again step & spare me the detail...
I'm not sharing a man not ever
While on your way... go tell her

She has you all to herself (maybe)
After awhile she'll know what I felt
How you get.... will be how you lose
Now I made my choice... fuck who you choose!

2006

"Never settle for less"

He Chose Me
By Miss Dee

What don't kill you makes you stronger
Once told, and yes life has showed
I continued to figure what it was I owed
Not taken much from the lessons bestowed

Until life drop the major bomb on me
Mother transformed to angel with her wings
At the time no understanding to these things
I just wanted to continue to cling

I was lost and fell into a deep dream
Life's trials not always what it seems
Questions running through my head
Further pain and more tears I had shed

As time progress the heartache faded
Adolescents advanced to adult hood invaded
Fragileness led the soul to clamp on first sight
Looking for the one "man" to just might

You see the REAL thing is a jealous man
How dare I ignore the fact in my life---so blind!
When he died and was betrayed by his own kind
Taking less then what I'm worth waiting in line

I have a gift that was given to me in prosperity
Not talking about materialistic but genuine sincerity
He chose me to see through his eyes
He chose me for life beyond the skies
With open arms I accept all of you
All these years you LORD brought me through

"Call on him and he will answer"

How Can Life Go On?
By Miss Dee

How can life go on?
When things are twisted things are gone
How can life be when I lost to my enemy?
I can never give him the justified pain he gave me

He holds nothing precious to him
He knows no love he hasn't any friend
He committed an immense sin
It doesn't matter how much I want to get even

I have to stay right for the remaining children
Needless to say, your life I could have stolen
For the price of taking my chosen
I will do what is right

I will not perform ungodly duties taking another's life
For a moment there I thought I just might
I will stand back and maintain life on track
God will do you Justice Yes indeed
You took what was precious
Maybe you were just jealous

Maybe that's my best guess
No... I just need to release this off my chest
An eye for and eye; you took what I held close inside
Now tables turn face what I faced
You are being dealt with, you are such a disgrace

You're inhuman to humanity
True lines of Futility, you bastard excuse my profanity
God has his vengeance, you will feel pain
As I pray never to feel this agony ever again

2007

"God sent a angel to teach the ungodly"

I had a Love so Strong

I had a love so strong
So
Strong!

Yes so strong that we met
When we were underage
Left our comfort zone
And reunited at a later date

When all the dreams and goals
Were running late
When lives have been intervened
When babies momma and daddy
Fled the seen....

Yes I had a Love so strong
So
So
Strong!

So strong we dived into each other
Like best friends and brothers...
Sentimental conversation
Was a great combination
To this future foundation

Yes I had a love so strong!

So Strong we married
And yes- his seed I wanted to carry
I wanted a little house on the prairie
A F. A. M. I. L. Y
But now I sigh...

I had A Love so strong!

So Strong!

So strong the pain didn't wait long
I am here crying to sad songs
I kept my faith and
Started reading Psalms!
I had A Love so Strong....

So
So strong that he left me alone
He ended up in another woman's home
A woman that hurts him without recognition
Now look at this awkward position

A woman's intuition
I knew before, I don't need to listen
You are weak and that's what she played on
How can we be when it's already gone

I had a Love So Strong!
So

So Strong that the marriage upheld
But my love I withheld
'cause I can forgive before I can forget
Stopped the game of rush and roulette
Now its time for you to sweat

I had a love so strong!

So strong that he promised me it all
But those were the words you said last fall
Seasons change and so did you
But as sure as the sky is blue
God will bring us through

I Had a Love So Strong!

"God heals all things"

I Want To
By: Miss Dee

You and I were in different leagues...
Yet; that did not matter....
Dazing into your eyes I became intrigued...
It was the suspense you kept me in...
When you would look at me...
I couldn't help but grin...

I want to ask...

That statement cannot be completed...
I know the feeling of being cheated...
We gain good conversation ...
As we are waiting, contemplating...
Infatuation is all up in here...
Truth be told, I am scared...

Unprepared for what's to come...
I just want to live a little...
Our time together has just begun...
I already have the one...
Still my thoughts continued to linger...

I've left things to commence...
I did not do this in good sense...
It was my body's lure...
My pounding heart...
You revive it for sure...

I want to ask...

Scenarios playing in the back of my mind...
Walk! Walk!
"Walk away from temptation"...
You and I can become a huge complication...

Trying to endure the sensation...
We have bypassed the flirtation...
What will I do in the mist of you...?
This is what you projected...
For me to fall, fall so hard for you...

As time reflected this energy...
Unexpected visionary of what could be...

I want to ask...

You want to give...
Give me things I never had...
I want to give in...
Give in to a man that understands...
Further you strive to be persistent...
The eclipse as...
My guard goes down...
I allow myself to be kissed...
Then I fell into his arms...
This is where I felt I belonged...

Wow....

I want to ask myself...
Was it worth it?

"Everything she missed at home"

*Is Blood Thicker?
By Miss Dee

My Situation that proved that blood is not
Play along relate to something I use to block
Ignored the verity of the Pathway that led to this
Family members that I can honestly say I don't miss

You read and very well may nod your head
But this is my perception of a family that went dead
Wasn't strong to say the least, its creation ate from a tree
That led to the poisoning of my mentality the became ones society

Which we knowingly know here today
All that my family could display, but aye
That's just what the say but I had to live out
In fear of what I am crammed with doubt

Blended DNA don't make it right nor okay
I tried to stray, detach myself and get the hell away
Found my way from a stranger that heeded my aide
That open doors; I made way not to falsify or betray

I can't identify with one that is comprised with that word "family"
Trust that my eyes will reveal to you strangely
It is what it is, mainly because those people gave up
Yes I said those, suppose you could walk my line-BUT

Envision your child life exposed to ones hatred, verbal, physical
Dreams being smashed, freedom being banned
Nightmares follow this same wrath of inhabitants that despise
Revolting, undesirable but hiding it all from the outside

In conclusion blood isn't anything if love's not present
Whether it's thicker or not, it needs to show on my clock
To be born in something makes it just that
Maybe someday the word "family" can mean more
Digest; was that apple good down to the core?

"A family can be beyond you own blood"

It's in My Walk

Many tried to make her fall;
Even after that she stands tall...
Holding her head up high
Always keeping her third eye...

Others are asking themselves...
Racking there brain cells...
Can't get close enough to tell...
You can try to sniff,
But you won't smell...

Dwell, yes dwell on the thought...
Monies an object...
&
I can't be bought...

The lessons been taught...
I walk with pride...
Therefore business stays my own...
In turn I can't be cloned...
One of kind...

This will never be again in this lifetime!
A sister of rhyme...
That has been on a grind...

"They say damn she fine...
That one there is a dime"

But Understand....

I am the lucky charm...
The pot of gold...
Escaped beyond the rainbow...
The first lady...
Born in nineteen eighty...

Producing power behind her walk...
A go getter...with no time to talk...
Opportunity has knocked...

The door is open...

I walk in
Freezing all negativity...
Enduring what's due to me prosperity!
My life I'm holding...
These haters are unfolding...
Give up for I am the chosen...

It's in my Walk!

"Confidence is not conceit love yourself"

*"Knocking Me"
By Miss Dee

This behavior is from the extreme Jealousy...
You can't honestly say you don't envy me...
Many years you hated my style...
Best to believe since I was a child...

To think your very own blood hates you...
Long while coming for me to see what's true...
You wish I were never born...
To you; another sibling was something to mourn...

I can remember the days...
You were begging for attention...
Being a middle child of dismay...
Then...I barely had comprehension...

At times you may act like you care...
You are faker than they come;
I was always aware...
I'll play your game as long as it takes...

Hopefully realization will determine....
This is not our fate...
My sister was supposed to be my friend...
The one I can hinge until the end...

Instead I got verbal abuse...
& I pleaded...Pleaded for a truce...

Will you ever see me as your sister?
You know I never ask to be here...
So let's end the family twister...
Am I making myself clear...?

See I'm tired of being the one to mend it...
My intelligence....
My demeanor...
You've already offended!

So many things you have done...
You lied...
You have made me cry...
All this was intentional...

This craze was anything but conventional...
That's what hurts the most...
Eight years too lengthy to be close...

All we had was each other...
After fifteen years you would never discover
...Didn't remember her last wish...
Prognosis; no you didn't...
...

Instead you allow money to decide
My father's gone and I let sleeping dog's lye...
Forgave, but never forgot...
Déjà vu...I remember the spot...
This woman... is out there to plot...

Grieving really blinded my vision...
Impaired my ability to make a good decision...
I heeded to the wise & loved her from a distance...
That's my only way for our coexistence...

My anger won't allow anymore...
I am all cried out...that's why I ended the war...
All these years of you being petty...
I moved on sweetie and your ass is on
The back burner already!

"Jealousy and envy a recipe for disaster"

Love Game

By Miss Dee

Okay.... sit down.... its time we had a talk

Listen or this time I swear I will walk

This urge---- I get when you are around

No wonder here----there is no solid

My heart skips a beat every time you appear...

At first sight lovely-   then your deadly spear...

Love games this time I'm in it to prevail...

Apparently you're there to make my heart quail...

This situation with you I must rectify...

Your intentions I.........Cannot identify...

For this I must rebel... rebel from you...

My eyes perceive that you are untrue...

Love games I have the Idea at hand...

Deceive me and make me love this man

You just seduced the most careful kind

Snuck right in a toyed with my mind

This intrusion was not even planned...

For you came and made yourself at ease...

Swung through my mind at a gentle breeze...

You are the beneficiary of this adventure....

Now, at last I get the big picture....

You...you cannot be what you claim

For that I hold all the blame...

Imposter....I know this is not love

These feelings have similarities ...

But can never be the real thing

Lust enables a lot of adversity...

Lust can never be trustworthy...

Lust

So long, games are now over!

"Lust can only substitute a short while"

My Destiny
By: Miss Dee

My prayers have been answered
The vision is no longer blurred...
For my father saw my heart...
& my cries he heard...

My waiting comes to a halt...
This man came out of no where...
Took my hand and led me out of despair...
A shine... was not just a glare...
Nothing I could compare...So rare

This friendship follows passion...
It's not your ordinary fashion...
As bodies and souls become in tact...
I react off the electricity...

You Bring...
Oh you bring...

Felicity!
My mind is at ease...
It's my soul you're after to please...
The power to make time freeze...

Let's love it is "You and I"
Like Stevie said "Ribbons in the Sky"
The contact has devotion high...

I'll sip you like wine...
Beautiful mature grapes from its vine...
A seed planted especially for me...
Heaven sent me divine destiny...

We'll love each other forever...
Give us Infinity!
Long Lasting...
Equals eternity...
You and I together!

"Soul mates are blessings from God"

My Fantasy

I'm alone in the dark
One candle lit
I'm in bliss
Thinking!

Sipping wine drinking...
Soft music caresses my intellect...
Dazing...the mind recollects
Drifting into the mist of you...

Can you feel me?

The subject... should I say
The object of my desire...
The effect of a woman wet...

Melting like ice cream...
Sweating off all this steam...
I feel your hands...
I am at your command...

Lick me; suckle me like butter pecan...
Unfasten my bra...
I am your picture to draw...

Can you feel me?

Swirling your tongue
Becoming
More! More! Sprung...
As you massage my back
I'm laying here in another world relaxed
She's hotter than wax!

I pull...you resist...
I insist...to feel your kiss
Pleaser...and teaser...
I'm boiling on overtime!

Can you feel me?

Ready to release...
This increase beat...
All down to my feet...
Sitting here in immediate need...

Climb in get between...

A king for a queen...
So the fits exquisite...
I submit...I'm shaking...
Take me

I clutch your manhood
Working those muscles...
I have you puzzled...

You're gasping for air...
I glance at your stare...
As I move
I'm back in formation...
You gave me motivation...

Back in forth...
South to north...

Can you feel me in my fantasy?

"Such vivid pictures of ones imagination"

My Intuition

By: Miss Dee

At times I tell myself to back off and chill…
They never understand the real until…
One would claim that's just your persona…
"She states it but she is full of drama"…

Half the time I'm always right…
When I am I see the fire ignite…
How can you blatantly deny…
Then act in shock utterly surprised…
Ignorance was something I always despised

Being an original player in this game…
Speaking wisdom to minds I proclaim…
Holding my head up high and not in shame…
Therefore I demand you say my name…

It's Dedrea…

Say it; say it until it's in your head…
A strong woman that birthed men with dreads…
The woven tapestry grows more thread…
Respect the grounds, hear what I said…

Follow no one's lead but my own…
Its takes a lot to sustain the throne…
Until my children proceed grown…
They will be able display what was shown…

Others foresee the casualties…
Runs, hides in text diaries…
She falls down but she always succeeds…
All rights, profits and proceeds…
They wonder why, and it's just me…
Digging and loving my territory…

I adore this position…
I nourish off my own ambition…
Making my own decisions…
Listening to my intuition….

"That voice is there so listen"

My Life

By: Miss Dee

My existence is for your name...
I attest that you are the air I breathe...
I am the picture, but you are the frame...
You make sense to me when things are strange...

The only thing that I perceive...
You're my island and summer breeze...

So...please never leave...

For you are brighter than the sun...
You're larger than the rain forest...
My medicine to make me numb...
The rhythm to the thumping drum...

So...please never leave...

See you keep me collected...
I died but in you I resurrected...
In me lies the mist of the lyric...
For you I will never quit...

Instead I'll represent...
I'll give not 50 but 100 percent...
Why...because you are my vent...

So...please never leave...

Leaving me will break infinity...
& I need you here in my vicinity...
The center of my universe...
You are the rib that gave birth...

This woman... but the girl came first...
I played with words and made it rhyme...
But after you I'm next in line...

So...please don't leave...

If you do there is no more me...
No more words for others to read...
& Immortal as words can be....
There is no destiny without my Poetry!

"God's gift to whom that will witness"

Obama
By Miss Dee

I can remember what my dad use to say...
A black man in office that would be the day...
Sadly he has passed on to greater things...
What he never saw, Obama will bring...

He has integrity
Stability for you and me...
He believes in education...
Not just for African Americans but;
All colors of the nation...

I know you all have frustration...
Eight years of bush too long in domination...

Obama will bring back the foundation;
That we all so desperately need...
Cutting cost that breaks middle class families...
Stopping mortgages from foreclosure...

He uncovered the indecent exposure;
Of a man that geared for revenge...
Who was really the one to apprehend?
Playing God to another culture's country...
Saying we need to agree to disagree...

We are blinded from the true focus...
Never mind that it's done deal...
He's richer than ever off us behind the wheel...
He owns Exxon and Shell...
Texaco, and Crown on the hill...

He's getting all that money...
Oh...and that stimulus check...
Was courtesy of China...
Fucking us harder than a vagina...

Raising the food price...
That doesn't suffice...
All money sent goes right back...

The Government is hustlers;
Lacking the distribution of crack...
Don't be surprised if there's another attack...
You hear it on the news...
It's always like that;
As we wait for a new president in office...

A black man can solve it...
Change is something needed indefinitely...
Obama has education count the degrees...
When McCain only completed a college course...
No the facts get down to the source...

Black man running, what could be worse?
McCain and his whack running mate...
Duplicating the last hard eight...
Did you watch the debate?
Wow...so much hate...

McCain does not even speak middle class...
The cost of living or the price of gas...
Oh, but Joe the plumber gets a free pass...
He makes over two hundred thousand...
You won't see him in public housing...

He said, "Joe I want you to stay rich"
Isn't that a son of a bitch...!
"Palin" spending government funds...
Media playing us acting shunned...

Bailing out big banks on Wall Street...
Using our damn tax money...
Yes our hard paying taxes...
There was never a state of decision...
The government needs supervision...
Vote November fourth...
It has to get better than any worse...
So watch out for the next presiding...
It will be Obama and Biden!

"Never give up now that change has come"

One More Glance
By Miss Dee

You're truly my life's joy
Your smile; your giggles that was my boy
Everything you did was to my surprise
You grew and learned before my eyes
Even though your dad laid out his goodbyes

You have to know you changed our lives
Everyday is a challenge for me to survive
I seem not to be able to rejoice
How I feel....I don't have a choice

I'm crying & I'm singing our song
The time passed it's been to long
I need a sign that will let me know its ok
The angels have opened the doors for your stay

Every morning of light
Every night of Darkness
I cry for you....

God hear my plea...
I followed your lead...
That man stole my seed...
That you planted in me...
Things have come to pass....
Now the Lord has its wrath...
But I want one more Glance
Give me that chance...I love you!

"Death does not mean forever"

"One Way Love"
By Miss Dee

You through bait I didn't bite...
Dark skin what I like, even good height...
But still...my fire you could not ignite...
My mentality was on the rebound...

The horror has already been drowned...
New insight here to be found
There is no way I can entertain you...
You still insisted to pursue...

One Way Love...

So eventually the guard flew...
Chance came for us two...
We talked for hours...
Glanced in a daze...
Wiping away tears...
Sheltering each others fears...

Furthermore I continued to crave...
Falling in love with your mind easy...
You're falling in lust...
My heart pending crush...
This design is not meant for us...

One Way Love...

Months pass...stones turn to glass...
My intuition puts you on blast...
I sense that brother has a scheme...
Needs plenty to help the self esteem...

Wanting to calm my imaginings...
You're like coffee without caffeine...
How many times in this scene...
Body betrayed by fragmented fantasies...

One Way Love...

Yet still I believe...
Not to give up so easily...
I cried and made pleads...
Your stimulated sexuality continues to breed...

So you say lets separate...

There's another you wish to penetrate...
This is the type of shit I hate...
In time I'll realize my own fate...

One Way Love...

These types come in all forms...
My fault to tamper with the norm...
The window braces for the storm...
I've been disappointed many times before...
I wish one way would have been my way!

My way to stray...
My way to betray...
But guess what...I am not that way...
I always stay...in harms way...

Bye One way Love!

"It really takes two for love to become true"

"Passion"
By Miss Dee

I thought a while back that I knew...
Knew what passion feels like to have...
To find out I never had.
Now I feel passion loved unconditionally...

I have a lot of flaws,
But you saw in me no cause...
U embraced my true self.
You took heed to my soul and helped.

I saw and felt true love,
Better than your average attraction...
More valuable then a night of satisfaction...
This is more than a trip to the movie;
A lot over here for you to perceive...

No such thing as standing still...
With you we always had adventure...
Now I can say I got the picture...
Yes; man you do deliver...

Committed promises let me know....
Your word is bond...
I'll remain calm...
I'm ready to endure the next level...

I thanked God for the settle of us two down....
Sign sealed delivered no one can come near it....
In a melody wrote for me to transmit...
This passion in my soul....
Has the highest roll...
The throne is waiting...
Blindly I am walking...
For eyesight is not needed for your grace....
There is nothing that could replace...

"Passion comes in all aspects of life"

Played Yourself
By Miss~Dee

You thought you knew it all
Enjoyed making others feel small
Never thought to look in the mirror
I eventually cried me a river

Keep Playing Yourself...

Growing tired of this view
My desires want a different pursuit...
My vitals show that you withdrew...
Recent pussy no longer new...

Keep Playing Yourself...

I had begun to feel...
& you instantly killed that thrill...
Insecurity in your head...
Ashamed for I made the most bread
Independently you could not produce...
You figure what's the use...
So frustration drags you down...

Keep Playing Yourself...

You can't manipulate...
It is I that constructs my fate...
You're here to complicate...
This here I must escape...

Sex...oh that's not enough...
Really...Call my bluff...
This phase is at its last days...
I don't want to belong to this maze...

Keep Playing Yourself...

I am not the hired help...
The easy free pleaser...
I am the over achiever...
The make you a believer...
The instant pain reliever...

You are not my receiver...
Look at the disguised golden retriever...
A good ass deceiver...

That now I must disperse...
Leaching on me you curse...
Love doesn't suppose to hurt...
Let me brush you off like dirt...

You Played Yourself!

"Rid yourself of the unworthy"

Reality
By Miss Dee

Awakening to you had me so content
My reality was hearing your voice
My doubts were there but I had no choice
We had beautiful conversations with one another

We both had our games putting up a cover
All the while we're becoming lovers
Closer than to loving brothers
Never imagined the title "You & I"

I was naive you were shy
Before I can say you already tried
I believe you're still soft for me there
Some Idea you wouldn't let me get near

Dazed by your presence enticed by your words
Control of the situation was what you preferred
Until I observed and no longer complied
My nose wow…you had me open wide

Despite our minor issues we still progress
Fortunate to exist, fortunate to be blessed
My thanks go to you, this I confess

You threw knowledge my way
I know my reasons for you to stay
Though our anger at times got the best
Just couldn't conquer love's test

That's what you have when in tune so tight
Love so strong, another made so right
That powerful energy was a bit much
Our souls clashing kept us in touch

We had no idea what was going on with our hearts
We fought it until finally we grew apart
Now our love has its own disguise… but why?
We gave up too easily love pass right by
We'll always have history our friendship is strong
Honestly that's where we originally belonged

"Facing the truth Alleviates Disappointant"
©2004

Reason for Cause

By Miss Dee

I lost a piece of my heart...
Had what most called an excellent start...
That is until she departs...
It was beyond my control...

Reason behind the cause...

A part of my soul gone...
Like a theft in the night...
Vanish went the light...
Silence of the scorned...
I'm torn, fought over...

Reason behind the Cause...

All eyes on her...
She's my daughter...
Well, she's my niece...
This tug of war needs to cease
This girl needs peace...

Reason behind the cause...

I continue to ponder...
Look at these vultures...
Am I apart of this culture...?

It's filled with hatred...
Catered with greed...
Who will listen to me?
My lost soul is emptied...

Reason behind the Cause

As a child drowns...
She begins to shutdown...
Darkness covers...
She pushers further...

Her outlet is here
This became clear
Vowed no more tears...

Embraced the fear...
Change and acceptance...
Adherent to the guidance...
His presence...its here!

He whispered in my ear...
So gentle so sincere...
"My dear I was always there"
"Your talent is within you"
"You just have to pursue"...

So I wrote all my hopes...
My way to rid and cope...
Then the vision aimed...
Poetry is its name...
I want you it proclaimed...

I give you the pen...
This gift is heaven sent...
For you it was meant...
This is your way to vent...

Paint a portrait...
My prophet, my POET!

"He gave the gift of a lifetime"

"SENSUAL LIPS"
By Miss Dee

To be up and beyond, to love unconditionally to be fond

You're unbelievable work to the eyes of the Lord

So what are you doing here, is it for me

The seas, the sweetness of thee...Come into me and learn...

Feeling motions moving oceans

Your love and devotion just the right potion

Can this be my right cup of tea, he bends his knee

To massage my feet, keep it coming so enchanting

Embrace my body with those sensual lips

Make way for my Jarring hips, I want you

To dip, dive explode inside, inside my soul

Lies passion and Intensity divine prophecy

A man that listens to the physique

It's so unique how the two bodies meet

Our souls combine as one, as we lay

To await the rise of the sun demonstration

Of the time consumed between a true companion

Harmonizing the eyes like the sun over our lives

Seemingly to my surprise a single kiss

Upon my gentle head love nourished

You have me thriving and abiding

Listening to his sensual lips inspiring my body

"Passion lies within you"

Sexual Pleasure

By Miss Dee

I like what he is mixing in this brew
You make me shiver by the thought of you
You moisten the panties just by your stare
Ooh when you're sexing softly pulling my hair

A kiss to the forehead links us to the bed
My touches, your tongue, following as I've led
Yet still... he's making love to my mind....Divine
I'm throwing gestures and the sex sign

I'm imagining me in that "ride" position
Your fingers working me overtime like a magician
Meanwhile I'm aching for you to get inside
I'm pulling you to slip in and slide..."wet and wild"

Have me shaking like child...Teasing me
As the sea pours...and further I endure..
Sucking my breast—moving down to finesse
Damn! Legs shivering clinging to you

My honey dew and his is not even through
He wipes the tears of my pleasure
I am that gem of his treasure
Moving from the bed to the dresser

Watching him do me the professor
Skilled in his game the pussycat tamed
I reach my climax...and the tone reflects
As the soft wet love of me tightens
He heightens and here it comes....SEXUAL PLEASURE

"Discover a deeper love"

Standing Still
By Miss Dee

This form I can't reconcile the situation
Destiny binds me to something I can't reach
Meanwhile my shoulders can't condone much more
Running petrified not knowing which door

Malicious mates trying to make war
Projects begun nothing near conclude
Racking my mind I must disperse this mood
My higher power wraps my soul
Break the evil that holds the control

I sense it lets make the correction
Go beyond life's work of reflection
Not going to apologize for being outspoken
Not going to become something to burden

In the eyes of others its ages long
How so wrong that business is my own
My surroundings no longer unknown
Resilient as always to the challenge faced
Time flies by not a minute left to waste

Surface the fear I must overcome
Ignore common trash their nothing but scum
Walk free exhale there is perception
Standing still no my direction

"Got to reach for the stars the sky is the limit"

Sweet Love
By: Miss Dee

Tasty comes to mind,
When I think of you
Let the summer breeze through
Join hands and embrace the truth...

Sweet Love...

Hold my heart; fill it with your love...
On this day cupid flies above...
As I wish he would join us two...

So freely grasping sweet honeydew...
Creating dreams to our own point of view...
Walking through soft sands on a beach...
Making funny faces enjoying our treats...

Sweet Love...

I will lay bright red rose pedals...
Leading you right to my level...
Endure the ecstasy of devotion...
Listening to sounds from the ocean...

Cupid has his bow and arrow...
Now here is my destined pharaoh...
A lifetime of you and I...
On your love I'm forever high...

Sweet Love...

Time is of no essence...
Expressing what we feel...
I say join with me in the creation of love
Receive thy soul in your heart...
Allow me to occupy my part...

The bridge of love has engaged
The emotions on our face displayed...
Overjoyed from a love made so great...
This is love when love is their fate...

Sweet love!

"Love is one of the most precious gifts"

Sweetest Joy
By Miss Dee

Your voice and laughter I can still hear
Unbelievable for some, to me very clear
I couldn't cope with the fact of your passing on
Listening & weeping to, I love you songs

Until maturity progressed my way
I finally saw that you are still with me
In my soul and definitely my heart
The Lord has told me you would never part

This forever bond that we will have
Not physical but I'm over being sad
My vision of you would not fade
Your love here, I feel it everyday

My spiritual light made so right
She had a duty to teach and love
God sent for her to fly above
Still here for me to embrace
Still saving me for heavens sake

Your image is still just as *vivid...*
Your smile next to the *sun...*
Your energy within the *wind...*
Your love I hold forever serene!

"The one that birthed this poet"

Swinging Hands
By Miss Dee

He spoke of love for her but expressed mental anguish
Claim to be a man but his love tarnished
She felt obligated to submit and serve
Obeying her vowels more than what he deserved

When he spoke, she was expected to jump
When she didn't, he proceeded to stump
Treating her as she were his child, not wife
Seasons change and this became her life

Enduring his rage and constant abuse
Family questions and she's looking obtuse
Really isn't that, just a stage of shock
Grasping the good memories others on block

Accepted the situation "he's just stressed out"
Knowingly can't help it, but you doubt
Reasons staying there are not enough
Being a single mother would be rough

Better that, then eventually ending up dead
Thinking-- you could do badly by yourself instead
In conclusion any abuse is not worth it to stay
When you do just gives him another way to betray!

"Love yourself enough to leave"

Taken Up Space!
By Miss Dee

15 yrs ago we crossed paths...
Things didn't add up so I did the math...
Fell in love with a mystifying person...
Matters evolve and my situation worsens...

Pregnant with your first born child...
I understood you needed to compile...
My guess you're still in denial...
Nine months is a long while...

Mature body's careless minds...
Now the art which we designed...
Fell upon the immature spirit...
Neglect surfaced, he's unable to commit...

Couldn't allow your life to be disrupted...
My love & kindness you've corrupted...
A miracle your seed up close...
You're in the vicinity but it's only for show...

There are lots of things for me to just let go....
Daddy, but a father is unknown....
His birth didn't stop your progression...
I was the one paying babysitters to make the lesson...

My anger eventually suppressed....
I know he has a father in Jesus...
Together we became mother and father...
You think even then he bothered?

Months turn into years away...
Missed the first step,
And words he chose to say...
Recognition of him became clear...
His absence will remain every year...

In time children learn...
Understand, comprehend...
Eventually he will have to accept...
Your reason you up and left...

Did not appreciate the image created of you
Instead you fled, like a coward
Enjoy being that wild flower...

"Single mothers doing it strong"

The Evil of This World
By Miss Dee

What the say is to live this straight life...
In time you fail and eventually see the light...
What bullshit foundation they have to offer...
I shall follow the lead of my founded father...

We work and strive for what we need...
All I see is these envious people in greed...
They have us here entwined in this organized game...
Chasing material things holds our race in shame...

This evil of the world...

Kids growing up by the vision on the screen...
Advertising the greatest achievement of a marine...
When their lives are intervened by gasoline...
I speak the truth of what these eyes have seen...

Frustrated our monies evaporate into fume...
Life as we know heading for doom...
Nine Eleven don't mistake it...its cruel...
Even after that he continued to play us for fool...

This evil of the world...

Many need to overcome this slavery of the mind...
The game is set for ploy societies bind...
We once had a dream where is it now...
Families together helping friends in need...

Now everyone out for self; chasing green...
While the white man laughs and enjoys the seen...
Look at those NIGGERS fighting and slaying...
Disappointed that the only jobs aren't paying...

This evil of the world...

We need to be praying and not betraying...
Teaching our daughter's and son's art of living...
Eliminating grudges and start forgiving...
Lend a hand and become uplifting...

Stop the evil of this world...

Stand my sister and brother walk with me...
Embrace each other honor the family tree...
Develop these teachings laid out from our ancestry...
Where we are now it's just a country... that's temporary...

Stop the evil of this world!

"No man knows the hour of Jesus Return"

The Guilty
By Miss Dee

Visually going back at our adolescents
Never anticipating you being on depressants
In my eyes you couldn't hurt a fly
Always had appreciation for life (so why?)

We had some tragic loses in our family
In turn you mastered being high daily
Your way I guess to rid the pain
Your choices made in vain

Not even the closes person to you could save
Never said... but God know you have misbehaved
Intentions to protect who would disrespect
The format made me question your intellect

If I could go back to that awful day
I would retract the words I'd chosen to say
Just to savage some part of your soul
You took life so easily so cold

Cowardly ran left auntie & mama betrayed
Still... love we had for you never would fade
Trying to pull together for catastrophe is here
Now we live life watching our surroundings in fear

Blinded to the fact 12 peers holds your fate
Testimony then evidence lurks in their mind
Wonders why they didn't have a confession signed
Wasted money & time case dismissed not this time

The way to redemption just got denied
No remorse for actions insult to injury
Guilty on all counts said the jury
In a blink of an eye regret pounded you
Thirty-Five to life-now your life is through!

"Decisions are made to be thought out"

The Struggle
By Miss Dee

I'm sitting here trying to find excuses
Yes, for all your damn misuses
I love you beyond meaning
You soul enjoying all the receiving

My heart on empty...but remained pleading
I sent enormous signs in your path
You sent me on the overwhelming wrath
It's like you silently laugh...

I felt your half baked love & inconsistency
I just wanted you to believe in me
I was not looking for another fantasy...

Oh God... again...

You had me embrace this mirage
My insecurity came to your massage
You tried to enmesh my heart...
You held a grip on my attention from the start

Now I feel this union coming to a closure
Don't hold your breath...I will hold my composure...
Women has been there as your reservoir
Well...this is something my heart deplores
Get out... don't let you ass hit the door...

Secondary involuntary to submit...
You're moving backwards, but can't admit...
In my circle lie individuals that are legit...
Vulgar activities I cannot permit...

So the struggle I must rid...
What you have done I forbid!

"Free your mind from negative people"

The Time is NOW!
By Miss Dee

The time has come to pass...
Longtime watching....
Like the hourglass...
Those have come and they have trespass....
My life getting by on chance...

But troubles never last...
Always was a matter of choice...
Therefore I reap the percussions...
My aftermath is sudden...

We learn from our mistakes...
Give a little and eventually take...
Love blindly, and suffer heartache...
Life is what you make...
You tell the real from the fake...

You become wiser with age...
Every sunrise it's a new day...
The pass never goes away...
Don't try you won't stray...

It's an open book guide...
Where I go next...I decide
Will I go under or will I hide...

The time is now....

Will I take the initiative...?
Will my dreams be fulfilled...?
This is what he instilled...

The gift of faith...
For the will theirs a way....
My skies no longer grey...
Humbled I gracefully say...

Give me abundance...
I traveled that dirt road...

Heeded what he bestowed...
For that my time is NOW!

"The road less traveled is the one to take"

The Wise & Confused
By Miss Dee

I remember when you said
Trust until it's broken...
Instead, I trust every word spoken...
Young dumb and confused...

I guess confusion is overrated...
People underestimated...
I'll eventually do me...
Unrelated tasks never sacred...

Goes in one ear...
Deleted from the other...
You win some you lose...
Always had something to prove...

You have to let go and let God...
I'm against all odds...
Embrace, don't run from change...
Don't use those words in vain...

All things come to pass...
Bad times never last...
It was hard being lower class...
I accepted change really fast...

Time waits for no man...
So get going have a plan...
You will fall but you can get up...
Through life you might encounter luck...

Understand the book of life...
The choice he gives to make it right...
Choices made and still able to repent...
New ones represent the present...

It shows what we actually learned...
Did we notice which way we turned...
Pray that the carriageway leads you home...
Are you the wise or confused?
Or are you the ones that will be accused...

"Only God can be our judge"

To Know Me

By Miss Dee

Knowing me did not come easily, but you tried...

Loving me could not come easier by my side

You explored my mind and not my body...

Endured the significance and not the taste...

Showered your love, so I can embrace...

Took you to levels you'd never perceive...

All because I love you and want you to achieve...

You know you have a back bone here when in need...

Raised up to be strong and stand on my own...

Followed a "Man's" lead as shown...

At times the love can be strict...

Being mindful avoids unnecessary conflict...

Don't mistake hard love for none at all

Cause loves still here standing tall

I'll trust until you give vital reason not

Without trust there is nothing we got

To know me is to know love....

To know love is to know the above....

Without him things would be different

We must lead & follow his intent

Time provided to know me had you by surprise

Love from me held you from future cry...

So to know me is a beautiful thing...

This woman here knows how to handle her King!

"Love is a beautiful selfless emotion"

Two Hearts One Man

By: Miss Dee

The life of a man that had two too many
Indulged in the essence of female flesh
It didn't matter to him more or less
Dipping and diving having unprotected sex

Married to one, the other is an unfinished conquest...
His title is battle and he unleashed his sperm
Two unborn children how do you come to terms
Pay attention and listen because he never learned

Protection for the home made but not with the one laid...
Out on a limb if the business it not concluded...
Abort the one but this argument is diluted...
With tears of fear loneliness became clear...

Left like a bad habit to adore the betrayed...
The scorned one called and confessed baby made...
Wife answers and how much she waited for this day...
My babies born and it's your husband's child I convey...

Desperate measures cause for desperate means...
Sorry said the lady I thought we were the team...
Your husband lied just to get in between...
I have his child and I need his support...
"Wife", says ok better take him to court...

My child is also in need...
And it's my husband's support that feeds...
Even though you played in the sheets...
I forgave him on all his misdeeds...

For the love of my family he will stay with me...
For your child I'm sorry that he deceived...
The husband gets the drift as he pleaded on his knees
Same ole story honey, you know it's not my seed...

Love blinded all is well in this house...
Kept secrets from his naive spouse...
The truth lies within his heart...
Which if ever came to light family would part....
His conscience would not let him sleep....
He knows another is out there whose heart now beats....

Years have passed....child grows up without a daddy to grasp....
Until that day when the lord took him...
Not a good way to find out through a distant friend...
All the time that was suppose to be Him and son...
His life has begun in another place which stunned...
Now the life he denied has no chance to rekindle...
Bet he wishes he never was the man that swindled...
To deny you own flesh in blood...now your heart floods...
Tremendous pain because you took your son in vain

"Lies have a way of surfacing"

Under this Control
By Miss Dee

She wasn't looking for another
Neither an affair nor a special friend...
Emptiness from home leads this situation to transcend...
She never was the type to be promiscuous...

It seems that convenience played its roll...
Her heart was there, only for him to console...
Their attraction was obvious, you know like on first sight...
Something in her eyes made this desirability ignite...

He saw what others seem to neglect...
This is the reason they minds connect...
She didn't have to display her emotional state...
With him it was ease not a hard out debate...

She knows that her other half is a factor...
Blinded by pain it didn't really matter...
When ones soul has been bruised...
When a love has been misused...

Vulnerability became deceptive...

This new found peace...
She stands from the man that new her least...
The conversation from loneliness...
Stimulates the desire to explore...

What the mind requests...
Her heart deplores...
Seized by the moment
Their bodies connect...

The intense anticipation it unfolds...
The sensation is growing influential...
I see time tables of lovers reverential...
He rejuvenated what was lost...
Just for the moment her pain paused...
For everything done there is a cause...
Then the cause became an affect...
Under this Control...

"Pain has a need to be comforted"

Untitled
By *Miss Dee*

Your love has had my heart on massage....
It sets off as a mirage...I thought I would stay in charge
But now I let you get inside....All this love here I must abide...
Your soft hand puts my body in a mist that needs to revive...

This lust you pass off as love gone in minutes...
Then off you go like an evicted tenant....
Your return heeds my invite.....Deep down
I know shit not right; your bark is as vicious as your bite...

Taken many pieces of me, sad & confused memories
Which personality is your true identity...I'm in search
Of my true destiny....I must not hold my breath for you
I must exhale & see what's true.....You don't deserve this
Title...and I defiantly don't need this battle....

I am precious to the heart...which means I need to part
Don't ever need to look back...Yeah; got to be like that
Please believe I don't want to hate you...No longer just us two
The part of you that thought you had me....Think different
That woman is gone....you ran her off...You had me at one
point...but I broke the fall...All and all your just plain dog...

At first I thought I had done wrong, this bullshit lasted too long
So be gone...not trying to here this sad song...
Just let things flow....maybe things were moving to slow...
That's another story to be told though....I must make the best
out this situation...I have another infatuation...Yes another relation...Oh
I can't receive congratulation...Its all good no need
to trip......This just explains why you're not worth shit!

"One never realizes what they have until it's gone"

What's Missing?
By Miss Dee

Dark symbolizing the vacancy in ones soul
Dimly walking grasping by sense and not by prospect
Fragile form that braces for the impact of neglect
Factual pretense unable to detect

Engaged in my fantasy unbelievable patience
Dodged the thoughts of a heart vacant
In need for filling of abundance in you
Reverts back to what's missing exactly mood

Provide the wants needs & desires
Emotion so strong nothing could devourer
Pretend me not when the mood waits
Ignoring all the possible stakes

Ceasing the moment as it's seen
Falling for you my body continues to lean
Divine intervention can't drift from the dream
I want to occupy, your eyes adhere my jeans

Let me reverse this energy back on me
Protection of Innocence as the island adjoining the sea
Focus on the inner beauty and talent not yet shown
Strong minds suppose to stand on their own

Hold together the faith you have inside
Rather have that then someone's denied
What's missing; my focus on life itself...
Combining shit that doesn't want to be felt
What's missing no- What's next.....

"Life is about changes don't be afraid"

*What's Justified
By Miss Dee

I gave you all of me
(That's Justified)
My soul is illuminating me to set you free
In my mind we're still connected
(That's justified)
Something told me this was not my find

Wondering were you ever mine body & soul
Surroundings played out deep and cold
My thoughts expressed to you getting old
(That's justified)
Four walls no way out, nothing here but a vacancy...

I was the one who let you in
(That's justified)
Now look here, it's my love you offend
Yeah...you thought you were cocky
Much to your surprise shit here is rocky

Here we go again this was meant to be
No-- bastard not me...and that's justified
Where was that instant chemistry?
My questions why, you could not deny

As we say, life goes on
(That's justified)
Thought this was another woman scorned
You want to undermine me & lay it down
I will keep the riches you can have the crown

You getting next to me... is yesterdays news
No...this shit here is not justified
Definitely not you and I...it died
You played with my heart & killed my pride
For that I cannot rekindle this unjustified love!

"Only the strong survive"

Printed in the United States
by Baker & Taylor Publisher Services